Hillary Rodham Clinton

by Tamra B. Orr

FIRST LADIES SECOND TO NONE

D0103018

PURPLE TOAD
PUBLISHING

FIRST LADIES Second to None

Abigail Adams
Dolley Madison
Edith Wilson
Eleanor Roosevelt
Hillary Rodham Clinton
Mary Todd Lincoln

Printing 1   2   3   4   5   6   7   8   9

Publisher's Cataloging-in-Publication Data
Orr, Tamra.
   Hillary Clinton / written by Tamra Orr.
   p. cm.
            Includes bibliographic references and index.
         ISBN 9781624691744
1. Clinton, Hillary Rodham—Juvenile literature. 2. Clinton, Bill, 1946—Juvenile literature. 3. Presidents' spouses—United States—Biography—Juvenile literature. I. Series: First Ladies : Second to None.
 E887.C55 2016
 973.929092
         Library of Congress Control Number: 2015941828
eBook ISBN: 9781624691751

Contents

Chapter One
NO WOMEN ALLOWED

The Situation Room was silent as President Obama and his closest security advisers held their breath. No one moved as they waited for word about the country's mission to find Osama bin Laden, who was hiding in Pakistan.

Secretary of State Hillary Clinton's heart was beating fast. Her worry and fear were written all over her face. Would the team of Navy Seals be successful? "My heart was in my throat," she told ABC News reporter Diane Sawyer, "because we were watching on the video screen what was happening."[1]

Moments later, the news came through. Terrorist Bin Laden was dead and the mission was a success. It was a tremendous relief, and for Hillary Clinton, a personal triumph as she had been one of the driving forces behind sending in the Seals.

It is hard to imagine today, knowing how intelligent and powerful she is, that anyone would look at Hillary Rodham Clinton and turn her away simply because she is a woman. However, that is just what happened to her—twice.

Concern and fear was on everyone's face as the people in the Situation Room waited for the news about the hunt for Osama bin Laden.

Young Hillary

The first time she was rejected, she was thirteen. Like most teenagers, she was exploring ideas for what career she might want one day. She loved playing sports, and after years of sparring with the dozens of neighborhood kids, she developed a strong sense of competition. She also loved to write. Perhaps she would become a journalist—or maybe a baseball player. Then she came up with her best idea yet: she wanted to be an astronaut.

Her interest was certainly understandable. President John F. Kennedy had fired the imagination of people of all ages when he proclaimed in 1961, "First, I believe that this nation should commit itself to achieving the goal, before this decade is out, of landing a man on the moon and returning him safely to the Earth." The Soviet Union had already kicked off the space race by launching *Sputnik* in 1957. This missile was the first manmade object to reach Earth's orbit. America panicked,

President Kennedy's speech about putting men on the moon to Congress, 1961

worried that they would come in second in this race to explore outer space. Within months, the U.S. government had created the National Aeronautics and Space Administration, or NASA. This federal agency focused on space exploration. Almost overnight, young people were imagining themselves blasting off into space and exploring the vastness of the universe. Hillary was one of those people.

NASA logo

"I wrote to NASA to ask how I could become an astronaut," she revealed in a speech in Washington in spring 2012. "And I got a response, which was, 'We're not interested in women astronauts.' " Hillary was shocked and disappointed. "Of course, there weren't any women astronauts, and NASA wrote me back and said there would not be any women astronauts. And I was just crestfallen," she added.[2]

In fact, there were female astronauts—just not in the United States. The first female astronaut to go into space was Valentina Tereshkova from Russia. In 1963, she was in space for almost three days, spending more hours in flight than all of the American astronauts put together. The United States did not send a woman into space until 1983—two decades later. Sally Ride had that honor, riding the *Challenger* into space as its mission specialist.

Years after her rejection, in 1975, Hillary faced the same kind of bias when she wanted to join the armed forces. When she was twenty-seven

Valentina Tereshkova and Sally Ride

In 1974, Hillary knew she wanted to get involved in serving her country—but how?

years old, already a law professor and soon to be married to Bill Clinton, she walked into a recruiting office and said she was interested in joining either the active forces or the reserves. The recruiter—a man several years younger than she—did not respond as she had hoped. "You're too old, you can't see and you're a woman," Hillary recalled. "It was not a very encouraging conversation," she added. "I decided, maybe I'll look for another way to serve my country."[3]

Experiences like these helped Hillary to become a passionate supporter of opportunities for women. "When we were growing up, there were just so many overt and implied obstacles to what young women could aspire to," she stated in an ABC interview. "There were certainly schools you couldn't go to, scholarships you couldn't apply for—jobs that were not available to you." Later, she added, "You really have to prepare. And you have to get knocked down, and you have to pick yourself up, and you have to keep going."[4]

Today, Hillary Clinton is one of the best-known political figures in the country. From her years as a lawyer to those spent as the country's first lady, and then as a presidential nominee, she has proven time and again that anything is possible—even if you're a woman.

The "Double Bind"

Over the years, Hillary Clinton has been praised and criticized—a big part of being in the public eye. In one story, she is labeled as passionate, dedicated, and assertive, while the next feature article labels her as aggressive, controlling, and power-hungry. If she shows too little emotion, she is called cold, but if she shows too much, she is suddenly judged unstable. As she stated in a speech in 1994, "There's that kind of double bind that women find themselves in. On the one hand, yes, be smart, stand up for yourself. On the other hand, don't offend anybody, don't step on toes, or you'll become somebody that nobody likes because you're too assertive."[5]

This type of commentary increased as the 2016 election was drawing closer. One 2014 editorial in *The Atlantic* stated, "Everywhere Hillary Clinton goes, a thousand cameras follow. Then she opens her mouth, and nothing happens." Another article states that "she would do enormous good for the country."[6]

Hillary Clinton is wise enough to find lessons in both the praise and criticism. She once stated, "Take criticism seriously, but not personally. If there is truth or merit in the criticism, try to learn from it. Otherwise, let it roll right off you."[7]

Cameras follow Hillary wherever she goes.

Chapter Two
MAKING HER MARK

The fish processing plant was cold, wet, and smelly. It might have been summer in Alaska, but inside the plant, it was miserable. It buzzed with the sound of conversation of young people who showed up from all over the country in search of seasonal work. Newbies were usually given the job of scooping out the innards of salmon—over and over. The process was known as "sliming fish."

It was a tough job, and Hillary Clinton and everyone else was expected to pull sixteen-hour shifts, seven days a week. As Hillary stood there sliming through the summer of 1969, she most likely did not imagine that one day she would be a well-known face in the White House. In a later speech she stated, "The best job I ever had in preparation for running for office was a job I had sliming fish. . . . I was in a salmon fishery where they brought in the salmon and they had some experts from Japan who . . . split the salmon open and took out the caviar and then they threw them in a big pile and I was there in hip boots with a spoon. And my job was to clean out everything else."[1]

Tough jobs like sliming fish taught Hillary how to endure unpleasant work when working for a larger goal.

Not only did the job expose Hillary to hard work, it also gave her an understanding of working conditions across America.

Hillary Diane Rodham was born on October 26, 1947, in Chicago, Illinois, to Hugh Rodham, the owner of a successful drapery fabric store, and Dorothy Emma Howell Rodham, a woman who worked hard to learn

Young Hillary was part of a loving and close family. Hillary's memories of her life in Park Ridge were happy ones.

from her own difficult childhood and pass those lessons on to her daughter. "You have to stand up for yourself," she told Hillary. Later, during her presidential campaign, Hillary thanked her mother for inspiring her. She described Dorothy as a woman "who never got a chance to go to college, who had a very difficult childhood, but who gave me a belief that I could do whatever I set my mind [to]."[2]

When Hillary was only three years old, the family moved to Park Ridge, Illinois, about 15 miles from downtown Chicago. Soon, brother Hugh Jr. joined the family, and four years later, brother Anthony was born. Hillary described her neighborhood this way: "Big elm trees lined the streets, meeting across the

The house in Park Ridge

top like a cathedral. Doors were left open, with kids running in and out of every house in the neighborhood."[3]

Almost every day after school, Hillary would join the other neighborhood kids to play games of chase-and-run, a combination of the classic games hide-and-seek and tag. "As with all of our games, the rules were elaborate and they were hammered out in long consultations on street corners," Hillary recalls in her memoirs. "It was how we spent countless hours."[4] She also spent time organizing food drives and being a Girl Scout.

Pursuing Politics

By the time Hillary was a teenager, she was already interested in politics. At thirteen, she was walking through her neighborhood trying to get people to vote for Richard Nixon for president. When she was fifteen, she heard a speech by civil rights leader Martin Luther King Jr. His words and his passion for protecting people's rights inspired her to learn more about social justice. At the age of eighteen, she was going door to door, working to get presidential nominee Barry Goldwater elected. She also helped

organize babysitting services for the children of migrant workers.

It did not surprise anyone when, after Hillary graduated from Maine South High School, she enrolled in Wellesley College as a political science major. To learn more about how the government worked, she served as a summer intern

Hillary Rodham

Park Ridge Girl Raps Brooke

Wellesley, Mass., June 1 (AP) — A Wellesley college student attacked remarks by Sen. Edward W. Brooke [R.- Mass.] today in a surprising reaction to a commencement address by Brooke at the college.

Miss Hillary Rodham, 21, of Park Ridge, Ill., an honor student and president of the Wellesley student government, told the 400 graduates and 2,000 spectators that Brooke's speech was similar to "a lot of the rhetoric we've been hearing for years."

Brooke Urges Nonviolence

Brooke had said the use of coercion as an instrument of change, resort to violent political action is anathema," Brooke said.

The appearance by Miss Rodham had been a scheduled part of the commencement exercise. It was the first time in the college's history that a student had spoken at a commencement ceremony.

Miss Rodham was selected by the graduating class as its voice in the graduation program. She had prepared remarks, but departed from them to reply to the Brooke speech.

"There has been very little of the action promised by that rhetoric," she said. "The entire tone of the speech was one that we found to be very discouraging.

Long Way from Goal

"We are a long way from the good society we seek," Brooke had said, "but not nearly so far as we would have been without the revolutionary changes which have marked private attitudes and public institutions."

Miss Rodham's retort included a call on her fellow students to heed legends scribbled on the walls of the Sorbonne in Paris by protesting French students. The signs urged young people to "Be realistic. Demand the impossible."

Hillary was featured in the newspaper when she challenged the viewpoints and statements of a senator who spoke at her college.

At Wellesley, Hillary got increasingly involved in politics and issues of social justice.

for the House Republican Conference. That experience deepened her passion for politics, but also changed which party she supported. After years of campaigning and supporting Republican candidates, Hillary became a Democrat—and would be from that point forward. She was also part of a winning team who appeared on television in the popular game show *College Bowl*. The series, which ran from 1950 to 1970, featured four-person teams from universities competing for scholarship money and fame.

When King was assassinated on April 4, 1968, Hillary knew she wanted to commit her life to stopping such national tragedies in any way she could. She was the first student in Wellesley's history to deliver a commencement speech. Her speech on May 31, 1969, was delivered so beautifully that she was given a standing ovation, plus she was featured in *Life* magazine as one of the country's most promising graduates.

Not one to spend the summer relaxing, Hillary instead worked her way across the state of Alaska. At the job she held in the fish-processing cannery in Valdez, she had the nerve to complain about how awful the working conditions were and was fired. Hillary also worked at Mount McKinley National Park washing dishes.

After Wellesley, Hillary went on to Yale Law School to earn her law degree. She was one of 27 women in a class of 235. She discovered a new interest there—children. She worked at the Yale Child Study Center and appeared in court many times to battle cases of child abuse. After she graduated from Yale, she continued this work by serving as the staff attorney for the Children's Defense Fund.

A Handsome Fellow Student

As busy as her life was during college, it was not so busy that Hillary did not notice a handsome young Yale student named William "Bill" Clinton. The two saw each other often on the college campus, and one day, Hillary decided to introduce herself. In an interview with Barbara Walters and *ABC News,* Hillary stated, "I still hadn't really met him, and I was sitting in the library, and he was standing just outside the door. He was looking at me, and I was looking at him. And I finally thought this was ridiculous, because every time I saw him on campus I just couldn't take my eyes off him, and he was always watching me. So I put my books down," she continued, "I walked out and I said, 'You know, if you're going to keep looking at me, and I'm going to keep looking back, we should know each other. I'm Hillary Rodham.' . . . It was an immediate attraction, and it was just a life changing experience to have met him."[5]

In 1974, Bill moved back to his home state of Arkansas, while Hillary moved on to Washington. He had already proposed to her several times, and she kept saying no. Instead, she became one of the 43 lawyers—

From the moment Hillary met her future husband, she knew her life was going to change.

Two future presidents?

and the only woman—to examine the guilt or innocence of President Nixon and his involvement in the Watergate scandal. Once Nixon resigned, Hillary's job came to an end. She passed the Arkansas bar exam, and moved to Arkansas to be with Bill. He was busy teaching law and running for Congress when she arrived.

Finally, one of Bill's proposals got the answer he wanted, and on October 11, 1975, Hillary and Bill were married. In an effort to keep her career separate from her husband's, Hillary kept her maiden name.

Hillary had already gone through some significant changes from tomboy in Illinois to powerful lawyer to new wife—but even more drastic changes were ahead.

Getting married was only one of the many changes in store for the Clintons.

Helping Children

The fact that Hillary had such a good childhood influenced her as a politician. Many of her programs, decisions, and speeches have centered on the importance of giving children a good education and helping families do all they can at home to teach and help their kids. "I had the best, most wonderful childhood: being outside, playing with my friends, being on my own, just loving life," she said. "When I was a kid in grade school, it was great. We were so independent, we were given so much freedom. But now it's impossible to imagine giving that to a child today. It's one of the great losses as a society. But I'm hopeful that we can regain the joy and experience of free play and neighborhood games that were taken for granted growing up in my generation. That would be one of the best gifts we could give our children."[6]

In 2013, Clinton joined a group called Next Generation and started the "Too Small to Fail" campaign. Studies have shown that kids from low-income families often have much smaller vocabularies than those from high-income backgrounds. This is known as "word gap." Having a strong vocabulary is an important key to being able to read and write well—and do well in school and beyond. Improving and expanding vocabularies can help students succeed and live happier childhoods—like Hillary's.

Changing a child's vocabulary has the ability to change that child's life.

TOO SMALL TO FAIL

Chapter Three

LIFE IN THE PUBLIC EYE

Taking a deep breath, Hillary held her arms up high, waving to the crowds. She was now the wife of the governor of Arkansas, and while it was exciting, it was also stressful. The last few years had brought change after change into her life. The changes were good ones, but adapting to each one was tiring. Putting that smile on her face and coping with the constant crowds was something Hillary would need to get used to—not just for that election day in 1978, but for many decades to come.

Can you imagine packing up everything you own and moving to a new state and a new house—all under the eyes of countless cameras and reporters? That is exactly what Hillary had to do after marrying Bill and moving to the state capital of Little Rock. It is easy to imagine the stress and the challenge of adapting to life in Arkansas and being the focus of attention. After only a year of marriage, when her husband had been elected state attorney general, she found herself in the public eye. "I didn't have an accent—a southern accent anyway—and you know, I'd worn blue jeans and work shirts and . . . big old sweaters all during law school, so I

Being in the spotlight was becoming part of her daily routine, but it was still a tough transition for Hillary.

did have some adjusting to do," she told ABC's Barbara Walters. "But I loved Arkansas, and the people of Arkansas were not only very good to me, but I made some of the best friends that I've ever made."[1]

In 1977, Hillary joined the Rose Law firm. Three years later, she became the firm's first female partner. Still interested in helping children, she helped establish the Arkansas Advocates for Children and Families, a group dedicated to protecting children, improving children's health, and fighting for educational choices for at-risk kids.

A New Job

Life changed again in 1979 when Bill went from Arkansas's attorney general to governor of the state. A matter of months later, in early 1980, Hillary

The cases she worked on at the Rose Law firm and the lessons they taught her helped Hillary in more ways than she could have imagined.

Becoming a mother reminded Hillary of why she worked so hard to help and protect the nation's children. It was a great honor to be named her state's woman of the year in 1984.

was given a brand-new job: mother. On February 27, Hillary and Bill's only child, Chelsea Victoria Clinton, was born. According to *U.S. News,* Chelsea was named after "Chelsea Morning," a song by her parents' favorite musician, Joni Mitchell.

Balancing marriage and parenthood took a great deal of her time, but Hillary still managed to stay active in politics. For twelve years, as the wife of the governor, she served as the state's First Lady. She continued to work at the law firm, focusing on helping children and families by serving on the boards of the Arkansas Children's Hospital and the Children's Defense Fund. In 1984, she was named Arkansas Woman of the Year.

During those years, Hillary found herself being studied and judged by the people

Hillary gives a speech as she accepts Woman of the Year in Arkansas.

and the media. While she had many fans, some people did not care for her. A number focused on the fact that, despite being Bill's wife and Chelsea's mother, Hillary still used her maiden name of Rodham. The public criticized her choices, and in 1981, that negativity affected Bill's job. He was not re-elected.

What should she do? Hillary decided to make a few changes. She adopted the Clinton name, and she changed how she dressed and behaved in public. The changes paid off. In 1983, Bill was re-elected as governor. For the next eight years, Hillary focused on improving education throughout the state. She set rules for classroom size and teacher testing. This dedication helped Bill Clinton become known as the "education governor."

Hillary's ongoing and dedicated involvement with children and education helped Arkansas become a stronger state.

First time as a First Lady, Hillary poses for an official photo of the new First Lady of Arkansas.

Beyond Arkansas

Hillary never stopped thinking of new ideas and fighting for new causes. Between 1982 and 1988, she was on the board of the New World Foundation, an organization that focuses on supporting communities and local leaders. She also served on the board of directors for several different companies, including Wal-Mart, TCBY (a yogurt company), and Lafarge (a cement maker). She was named Arkansas Woman of the Year in 1983, Arkansas Young Mother of the Year in 1984, and to the *National Law Journal's* list of the 100 most influential lawyers in the U.S. in both 1988 and 1991.

For a dozen years, Hillary did all she could for the people in the state of Arkansas and to support her husband's five terms as governor. She was also standing right by his side when he made the announcement that grabbed the attention of the nation: Bill Clinton was running for President of the United States.

The road to the White House was not smooth or easy for the Clintons. In 1992, Bill was accused of having a relationship with a woman named Gennifer Flowers. It was Hillary's strong support of her husband that made

Despite embarrassing accusations, the Clinton campaign forged ahead, working to win the confidence and trust of Americans during the election.

it possible for him to continue his campaign—and eventually be elected president. Despite rumors and criticism, Hillary proudly endured interviews, cameras, and being in the spotlight with complete confidence that her husband was an honest man, worthy of becoming the country's 42nd president. Bill's election in 1993 was largely due to the strength and dedication of Hillary, a loving and supportive wife.

Equal Rights for Women

One of the issues Hillary has most deeply cared about over the years is equal rights for women—at home, in the workplace, and in politics. The issue of her last name reflected her ideals. Many reporters commented on the fact that she continued to use her maiden name even after she was married. In response, Hillary explained, "I don't have to change my name. I've been Mrs. Bill Clinton. I kept the professional name Hillary Rodham Clinton in my law practice, but now I'm going to be taking a leave of absence from the law firm to campaign full-time for Bill and I'll be Mrs. Bill Clinton."[2]

In 2014, Hillary brought up women's rights even more, campaigning for equal pay for women. She stated, "Too many women in too many countries speak the same language—of silence."[3] She has also started a new program for helping disadvantaged girls go to secondary school. As Adrienne Elrod, a communications director and Hillary supporter, once said, "Hillary Clinton believes that equal opportunity and success for women and girls builds a better future for all."[4]

Whether as a lawyer, a governor's wife, or the first lady, Hillary has continued to speak up for women's rights in the U.S.

Chapter Four
IN THE WHITE HOUSE

If Hillary had been overwhelmed by being in the public eye before, her husband's presidential campaign and inauguration made her well-known not only throughout the country, but throughout the world. Her picture was taken everywhere she went, and commentators analyzed everything she did, from what she wore to how she cut her hair. She once told a reporter, "If I want to knock a story off the front page, I just change my hairstyle."[1]

In January 1993, the Clintons moved into the White House in Washington, and Hillary went from being the first lady of Arkansas to FLOTUS—First Lady of the United States. The new position did not mean that she stood back and let her husband do all the hard work, however. Hillary was given her own office in the White House's West Wing. Knowing that his wife was experienced, smart, and ambitious, Bill named Hillary as the head of a task force that would research America's health care problems and find answers for them.

The next few years were challenging. Hillary worked hard studying health care issues, touring the country, talking to people, and gathering a

Bill and Hillary were delighted when Bill won the presidential election, even though they knew there would be many challenges waiting ahead.

Although Hillary was passionate about her health care plan in 1993, it ended up damaging her reputation rather than supporting it.

group of advisers to help her draft a plan. In the end, her health care plan was so complicated it did not get the government backing and public support it needed. The entire plan was dropped, and Hillary's image with the American people was damaged. She was seen as too controlling, and taking too large a role for a first lady.

Changing Focus

In 1995, Hillary took up the pen. She began writing a weekly newspaper column called *Talking It Over.* The column covered topics involving the importance of providing after-school activities for children, reducing air pollution in schools, and spending more time together as families. In her April 20, 1998, column she wrote, "It's time to turn the TV off and spend more time with our kids. Time is what every child wants and needs. We live in a fast world, where slowing down to spend time with our families is hard to do—unless we make it a priority. Our children are our greatest gift, our greatest responsibility, our greatest test."[2]

The next year, Hillary found herself on *The New York Times* bestseller list with her book *It Takes a Village and Other Lessons Children Teach Us*. It sold millions of copies within the first few weeks. The book focused on the need for every child to be raised by a loving and supportive family, community, and educational system. The title was based on the saying, "It takes a village to raise a child." In a speech in August 1996, Hillary stated, "I chose that old African proverb to title my book because it offers a timeless reminder that children will thrive only if their families thrive and if the whole of society cares enough to provide for them."[3] In 1997, Hillary won a Grammy for Best Spoken Word Album for her recording of her book.

Hillary had spent years of her life working to help children, and in 1997 she returned to that focus. Combining all she had learned about insurance choices with her passion for protecting children, she created the State Children's Health Insurance

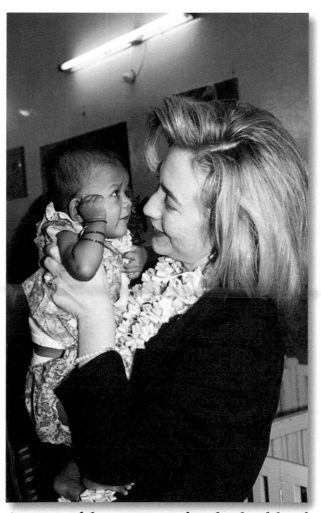

As part of her concern for the health of the country's children, Hillary often visited hospitals across the nation.

Talking to children in school rooms across the U.S. helped keep Hillary aware of important issues.

Program (commonly called CHIP). Through her new program, she promoted the importance of routine immunizations for kids, and made sure money was provided to research conditions like childhood asthma. She also helped pass legislation to protect children in abusive foster and adoptive family situations. Along with Bill, she hosted the White House Conference on Early Childhood Development and Learning, as well as the White House Conference on Child Care.

With Hillary's focus on helping children and families, she did a great deal of traveling, going to more than 80 countries and serving as a goodwill

Hillary visited many other countries in order to speak to women and children, and her daughter Chelsea often accompanied her.

ambassador. She spoke to endless audiences about women's rights and equality, as well as education for all young people.

Another Scandal

Despite Hillary's dedication to helping others, she continued to face criticism from the public. She was the most vocal and involved first lady that Americans had ever seen, and not everyone was ready for that change.

In 1995, the Clintons faced another scandal like the one with Gennifer Flowers years before. Bill was accused of lying under oath about his relationship with another young woman. He faced impeachment for telling that lie. It was Hillary's defense of her husband that, once again, helped him get through the negative press. It also won Hillary many fans across the country. It was just in time too, because Hillary had a new goal in mind.

The Clintons continued to smile and wave at their supporters even as they weathered the accusations of lying.

America got the chance to see another side of Hillary when she was elected Senator of New York.

On to the Senate

It did not surprise anyone that Hillary wanted to be more involved in politics. In 1999, she began campaigning for a U.S. Senate seat from New York. After sixteen months, she was elected. She was the first female senator in New York's history. She was also the first FLOTUS to be elected to national office. In 2003, she published another book. Titled *Living History,* the book detailed her years as a wife, mother, and politician. In 2006, she was easily re-elected to a second term as New York senator.

During her time as senator, Hillary served on many different boards concerning issues such as health, education, labor, aging, and quality of life for people who have served in the armed forces and their families. Hillary's plans did not stop at being senator, however. In early 2007, she made the announcement that many people had been waiting for: she was running for U.S. president in the next election. For the first time in history, the FLOTUS was setting her sights on becoming the POTUS (President of the United States).

Family Values

Over her years in politics, Hillary has spoken out about the many roles women play in today's culture and their struggle to keep them in balance. In the past, she has stated, "Our lives are a mixture of different roles. Most of us are doing the best we can to find whatever the right balance is. . . . For me, that balance is family, work, and service."[4]

She has passed her values on to daughter Chelsea, who is vice chairperson for the Bill, Hillary & Chelsea Clinton Foundation. The foundation is focused on improving people's lives worldwide. According to its web site, "Whether it's improving global health, increasing opportunity for women and girls, reducing childhood obesity and preventable diseases, creating economic opportunity and growth, or helping communities address the effects of climate change, we keep score by the lives that are saved or improved."[5] It continues the nonprofit work Hillary began in the 1970s.

Chelsea and her husband, Marc Mezvinsky, announced the birth of their daughter Charlotte Clinton Mezvinsky on September 26, 2014. "I just hope that I will be as good a mom to my child and hopefully children as my mom was to me," Chelsea said.[6]

Chelsea Clinton

Chapter Five
A PRESIDENTIAL FUTURE?

This is not going to be an easy act, thought Hillary. She would have to stay calm, cool, and collected or an important man might get in terrible trouble.

As Secretary of State, she was in China in May 2012 on a diplomatic mission. Officially she was there to talk about economic and security issues with China's President Hu Jintao. The trick was to appear as if nothing else was going on. In reality, behind the scenes, Hillary was also negotiating for the release of Chen Guangcheng, a blind lawyer and activist being held in China against his will.

After Chen was safely on American grounds, Hillary finally took a deep breath. "The image of Chen, blind and injured, seeking through that dangerous night for the one place he knew stood for freedom and opportunity—the embassy of the United States," wrote Hillary in her memoirs, "reminds us of our responsibility to make sure our country remains the beacon for dissidents and dreamers all over the world."[1]

Years before her success as Secretary of State, Hillary had another goal in mind. "I'm in and I'm in to win," she announced on her campaign web site in early 2007.[2] For months, people had hoped and/or suspected she would

When Hillary stepped down as Secretary of State, the smile on her face was a clue that she had bigger goals just around the corner.

Hillary easily won many of the states during her first run at the presidential primary.

run as the Democratic nominee for president in the 2008 election. They were right! Hillary had her sights set on becoming the next president, after her husband. "I grew up in a middle class family in the middle of America, and we believed in that promise [of America]." She added, "I still do. I've spent my entire life trying to make good on it, whether it was fighting for women's basic rights or children's basic health care, protecting our social security or protecting our soldiers."[3]

During her campaign, Hillary focused on becoming the first female presidential nominee. She appeared many times in front of crowds with her mother and daughter on either side of her. This definitely appealed to women voters. She also had Bill join her on the campaign, but some of his comments and speeches ended up hurting her presidential chances rather than helping them. Although she was a top runner for the early months of the race, her lead began to shrink after she lost a number of debates with competitors Barack Obama and John Edwards.

By summer, Hillary ended her campaign. It was clear that nominee Barack Obama would be the Democratic contender in the election. The two politicians had been involved in 22 debates over 16 months. In a speech to all of her fans and supporters, Hillary stated, "You can be so proud that, from now on, it will be unremarkable for a woman to win primary state victories, unremarkable to have a woman in a close race to be our nominee, unremarkable to think that a woman can be the president of the United States. To those who are disappointed that we couldn't go all the way, especially the young people who put so much into this campaign, it would break my heart if, in falling short of my goal, I in any way discouraged any of you from pursuing yours."[4]

A New Job

President Obama remembered the grit, strength, and talent of his election competition, and soon after being elected, he nominated Hillary as the country's secretary of state. On January 21, 2009, Hillary Rodham Clinton officially became the 67th U.S. Secretary of State. It was another first for the nation, as Hillary was the first former first lady to serve on a presidential cabinet.

Hillary enjoyed her new job. She continued to fight for women's rights and human rights. She traveled to 112 countries, covering almost one million miles. Her job ended in 2013, and then she decided to do something she really needed: she relaxed for a while. She and Bill took a vacation in New York. In an interview with *The Huffington Post,* she said, "I've had the most enjoyable and restful time, by my standards. . . . We live in a little renovated farmhouse north of New York City, we have three dogs, we go for long walks. . . . It's just been wonderful being able to breathe deeply, take yoga, learn to breathe better and all that."[5]

What is Next?

On August 1, 2010, Hillary Clinton added another title to her long list: mother-in-law. Chelsea Clinton married investment banker Marc Mezvinsky. Then, on September 26, 2014, the Clintons welcomed their first grandchild, Charlotte Clinton Mezvinsky. Being grandma was a thrill for Hillary, and she postponed announcing her next plans so that she would have time to enjoy Charlotte. "I want to see what [being a grandparent] feels like," she told Charlie Rose in an interview for PBS. "I want to really be present, as I meet this . . . new person in our family."[6]

That year also saw the birth of another book, *Hard Choices: A Memoir*. It focused on her years as secretary of state. In the introduction she writes, "All of us face hard choices in our lives. Life is about making such choices. Our choices and how we handle them shape the people we become."[7]

Rumors about what would be next for Hillary were common in Washington—and throughout the rest of the country. Many people were eager to see her run for president in the 2016 election, including President Obama. Calling Hillary a personal friend, Obama stated in an interview with *ABC News* that Hillary would make a great president, even if she had some different opinions than he did. "She's not going to agree with me on everything," he said. "And, you know, one of the benefits of running for president is you can stake out your own positions."[8]

In September 2014, Hillary told the public she would make an official decision about running for president in 2016 "after the first of the year." January 2015 came and went—without any announcement. So did February and March. Finally, in mid-April, Hillary posted a video message to her campaign web site, saying, "Everyday Americans need a champion and I want to be that champion." There is little doubt that she will have many people ready to campaign and vote for her. All in all, that's not bad for a girl who was told she couldn't be an astronaut or join the armed forces.

Hillary was off and running . . . again.

Hillary Clinton
2016

"An Extraordinary Role"

During her campaign for presidency in 2008, Hillary finally conceded to contender Barack Obama. She told the crowd, "Now, think how much progress we've already made. When we first started, people everywhere asked the same questions. Could a woman really serve as commander in chief? Well, I think we answered that one. Could an African American really be our president? And Senator Obama has answered that one." Clinton and Obama worked well in the White House together, although they often disagreed on policies and decisions.

On January 27, 2013, Clinton and Obama were brought together—at their request—on the television show *60 Minutes* for a brief interview. The purpose of the interview quickly became apparent: they wanted the country to see that they were friends who appreciated the chance to work together. President Obama called Hillary "one of the finest secretaries of state we've had. . . . I want the country to appreciate just what an extraordinary role she's played during the course of my administration and a lot of the successes we've had internationally have been because of her hard work." The feelings were clearly mutual. Hillary added, ". . . this has been just an extraordinary opportunity to work with him as a partner and friend, to do our very best on behalf of this country we both love."[9]

Opponents in 2008, Barack Obama and Hillary Clinton grew to respect and trust each other.

1947   Hillary Rodham is born in Chicago, Illinois.

1962   Hillary meets Rev. Martin Luther King Jr. at a youth group event.

1964   Hillary campaigns for presidential candidate Barry Goldwater.

1965   Hillary graduates from high school and attends Wellesley College.

1969   Hillary graduates from Wellesley College, gives a controversial graduation speech, and enrolls at Yale Law School.

1970   Hillary meets Bill Clinton and works at Children's Defense Fund.

1972   Hillary works on Senator George McGovern's presidential campaign.

1973   Hillary graduates from Yale.

1974   Hillary is appointed to Staff of House Judiciary Committee; she teaches at University of Arkansas Law School.

1975   Hillary marries Bill Clinton.

1976   Hillary joins the Rose Law Firm.

1977   Hillary is appointed to board of the Legal Services Corporation by President Jimmy Carter.

1979–1981 Hillary becomes the First Lady of Arkansas when Bill is elected governor.

1980   Daughter Chelsea is born.

1983   Hillary is appointed head of the Arkansas Education Standards Committee.

1983–1992   Hillary serves as First Lady of Arkansas for Bill's additional terms as governor.

1993   Hillary becomes the First Lady of the United States when Bill is elected President, and she is appointed chair of the health care task force.

1994   Hillary is awarded the Living Legacy Award.

1996   Hillary publishes *It Takes a Village: And Other Lessons Our Children Teach Us*.

1997   Hillary wins a Grammy Award for Best Spoken Word Album for *It Takes a Village*.

1999   She is awarded a Lifetime Achievement Award.

2000   Hillary is elected to U.S. Senate from New York. She serves from 2001 to 2009.

2003   Hillary publishes her memoirs, *Living History*.

2005   Hillary is inducted into the National Women's Hall of Fame.

2007   She announces her campaign for presidency.

2009   Hillary is nominated as 67th U.S. Secretary of State by President Barack Obama. She serves until 2013.

2014   Hillary becomes a grandmother when Chelsea has a daughter, Charlotte Clinton Mezvinsky. Hillary also publishes *Hard Choices: A Memoir*.

2015   She decides to run for president.

Chapter 1

1. "The Hillary Clinton Interview: 21 Revealing Quotes," *ABC News,* June 9, 2014, http://abcnews. go.com/Politics/hillary-clinton-interview-21-revealing-quotes/story?id=24064953&page=2

2. Charlie Spiering, "Hillary Clinton: NASA Said I Couldn't Go to Space," *Washington Examiner,* March 21, 2012, http://www.washingtonexaminer.com/hillary-clinton-nasa-said-i-couldntgo-to-space/article/1189121

3. Maureen Dowd, "Hillary Clinton Says She Once Tried to Be Marine," *The New York Times,* June 15,1994. http://www.nytimes.com/1994/06/15/us/hillary-clinton-says-she-once-tried-to-be-marine.html

4. "The Hillary Clinton Interview."

5. Larry Jordan, "The Real Hillary Clinton," *Midwest Today,* June 1994, http://www. midtod.com/highlights/hillary.phtml

6. Molly Ball, "Does Hillary Clinton Have Anything to Say?" *The Atlantic,* September 19, 2014, http://www.theatlantic.com/politics/archive/2014/09/does-hillary-clinton-have-anythingto-say/380483/

7. Sarah Vermunt, "Hillary Clinton's Advice on Taking Criticism," *The Huffington Post,* July 7, 2013, http://www.huffingtonpost.ca/sarah-vermunt/how-to-take-criticism_b_3595074.html

Chapter 2

1. Jon Trott, "Hillary Clinton to Wyoming: 'My Best Job Was Sliming Fish.' " *Blue Christian on a Red Background,* March 8, 2008, http://bluechristian.blogspot.com/2008/03/hillary-clinton-towyoming-my-best-job.html

2. "Biography: Hillary Rodham Clinton." PBS: *American Experience,* n.d., http://www.pbs.org/wgbh/americanexperience/features/biography/clinton-hillary

3. Peter Gray. "Hillary Clinton's and My Wonderful Childhoods," *Psychology Today,* July 22, 2009. https://www.psychologytoday.com/blog/freedom-learn/200907/hillary-clinton-s-and-mywonderful- childhoods

4. Ibid.

5. "Hillary and Bill: 'Immediate Attraction.'" *ABC News,* June 9, 2003, http://abcnews.go.com/2020/story?id=123702

6. Gray.

Chapter 3

1. "Hillary and Bill: 'Immediate Attraction.'" *ABC News,* June 9, 2003, http://abcnews.go.com/2020/story?id=123702

2. Michael Kelly, "Again: It's Hillary Rodham Clinton. Got That?" *The New York Times,* February 14, 1993, http://www.nytimes.com/1993/02/14/us/again-it-s-hillary-rodham-clinton-got-that.html

3. Todd Purdum, "Hillary Clinton Finding a New Voice," *The New York Times,* March 30, 1995. http://www.nytimes.com/1995/03/30/world/hillary-clinton-fi nding-a-new-voice.html

4. Amie Parnes, "Hillary Clinton Puts Women's Rights at Center of Her Agenda," *The Hill,* September 27, 2014. http://thehill.com/homenews/campaign/219058-hillary-clinton-puts-womens-rightsat-center-of-her-agenda

Chapter 4

1. Alyson Walsh, "The Hillary Clinton Look: Power Hair, Pantsuits and Practicality," *The Guardian,* April 15, 2015, http://www.theguardian.com/fashion/2015/apr/15/the-hillary-clinton-look-powerhair-pantsuits-and-practicality

2. Hillary Clinton, "Talking It Over," *On the Issues,* April 20, 1998. http://www.ontheissues.org/Archive/Talking_It_Over_Hillary_Clinton.htm

3. Hillary Clinton, "Text of Hillary Clinton Speech," Associated Press, August 27, 1996. http://www.happinessonline.org/LoveAndHelpChildren/p12.htm

4. "First Ladies: Hillary Rodham Clinton," White House.gov, n.d., https://www.whitehouse.gov/1600/first-ladies/hillaryclinton

5. Clinton Foundation, "About Us," n.d., https://www.clintonfoundation.org/about

6. Ken Thomas, "New Mom Chelsea Clinton Celebrates Baby Daughter," *Dallas News,* September 27, 2014, http://www.dallasnews.com/news/local-news/20140927-new-mom-chelsea-clinton-celebratesbaby-daughter.ece

Chapter 5

1. Hillary Clinton, *Hard Choices: A Memoir* (New York: Simon & Schuster, 2014).

2. "Clinton: "I'm In, and I'm In to Win,' " *NBC News,* January 21, 2007. http://www.nbcnews.com/id/16720167/ns/politics/t/clinton-im-im-win/#.VV5BYU_BzGc

3. Hillary Clinton, "Video Transcript: Presidential Exploratory Committee Announcement," January 20, 2007, http://www.4president.org/speeches/hillary2008announcement.htm

4. "Hillary Clinton Endorses Barack Obama," video transcript, *The New York Times,* June 7, 2008, http://www.nytimes.com/2008/06/07/us/politics/07text-clinton.html

5. Igor Bobic, "Hillary Clinton Describes How She Unplugged After State Department Job," *The Huffington Post,* July 5, 2014. http://www.huffingtonpost.com/2014/07/05/hillary-clintonthrive_n_5560491.html

6. Teddy Amenabar, "Hillary Clinton Said She Was 'Thinking' About a 2016 Run. So. Many. Times." *NBC News,* April 10, 2015, http://www.nbcnews.com/politics/first-read/hillary-clinton-said-she-was-thinking-about-2016-run-so-n338906

7. Clinton, *Hard Choices.*

8. "Obama, Hillary Clinton Meet at White House but Details Are Few." *Reuters,* December 3, 2014. http://www.reuters.com/article/2014/12/03/us-usa-politics-obama-clintonid USKCN0JH2NJ20141203

9. Steve Kroft, "Obama and Clinton: The *60 Minutes* Interview." *CBS News,* January 28, 2013, http://www.cbsnews.com/news/obama-and-clinton-the-60-minutes-interview/

Works Consulted

Adams, Myra. "16 Reasons Why Hillary Clinton Will Win 2016." *The Daily Beast,* August 3, 2012. http://www.dailymail.co.uk/news/article-2805405/Hillary-uses-granddaughter-campaign-speech-s-not-month-old.html

Agence France-Presse. "Hillary Clinton Uses Books to Defend Role in Chen Guangcheng's Release." *The South China Morning Post,* June 11, 2014. http://www.scmp.com/news/world/article/1529434/hillary-clinton-uses-book-defend-role-chen-guangchengs-release

American Experience, "Biography: Hillary Rodham Clinton." http://www.pbs.org/wgbh/americanexperience/features/biography/clinton-hillary/

Ball, Molly. "Does Hillary Clinton Have Anything to Say?" *The Atlantic,* September 19, 2014. http://www.theatlantic.com/politics/archive/2014/09/does-hillary-clinton-have-anything-to-say/380483/

Balz, Dan. "Hillary Clinton Opens Presidential Bid." *The Washington Post*, January 21, 2007. http://www.washingtonpost.com/wp-dyn/content/article/2007/01/20/AR2007012000426.html

Bell, Ben. "President Obama: American People Want 'New Car Smell' in 2016 Campaign." ABC News, November 23, 2014. http://abcnews.go.com/Politics/president-obama-american-people-car-smell-2016-campaign/story?id=27108324

Bidwell, Allie. "Hillary Clinton Pushes Early Childhood Development." *U.S. News,* November 20, 2013. http://www.usnews.com/news/articles/2013/11/20/hillary-clinton-pushes-early-childhood-development

Bobic, Igor. "Hillary Clinton Describes How She Unplugged After State Department Job." *Huffington Post,* July 5, 2014. http://www.huffingtonpost.com/2014/07/05/hillary-clinton-thrive_n_5560491.html

Bradley, Tahman. "Hillary Clinton the Tomboy and Her 'Ah-Ha' Moment." ABC News, March 30, 2009. http://abcnews.go.com/blogs/politics/2009/03/hillary-clinton-7/

Chambers, Francesca. "Hillary Is Already Using Charlotte Clinton Mezvinsky as a Campaign Tool—and She's Not Even a Month Old." *The Daily Mail,* October 23, 2014. http://www.dailymail.co.uk/news/article-2805405/Hillary-uses-granddaughter-campaign-speech-s-not-month-old.html

Chen Guangcheng. "Chen Guangcheng: Still Waiting on China to Honor Its Pledges." *The Washington Post,* June 24, 2014. http://www.washingtonpost.com/opinions/chen-guangcheng-still-waiting-on-china-to-honor-its-pledges/2014/06/24/7e52ec4e-fb04-11e3-b1f4-8e77c632c07b_story.html

Clinton, Hillary. "Talking It Over." *On the Issues,* April 20, 1998. http://www.ontheissues.org/Archive/Talking_It_Over_Hillary_Clinton.htm

Clinton, Hillary. "Text of Hillary Clinton Speech." August 27, 1996. http://www.happinessonline.org/LoveAndHelpChildren/p12.htm

Dowd, Maureen. "Hillary Clinton Says She Once Tried to Be Marine." *The New York Times,* June 15, 1994, http://www.nytimes.com/1994/06/15/us/hillary-clinton-says-she-once-tried-to-be-marine.html

Fox News Latino. "Democratic Rising Star Julian Castro Praises Hillary Clinton." Fox News, January 13, 2015. http://latino.foxnews.com/latino/politics/2015/01/13/democratic-rising-star-julian-castro-praises-hillary-clinton/

Good, Chris. "The Hillary Clinton Interview: 21 Revealing Quotes." ABC News, June 9, 2014. http://abcnews.go.com/Politics/hillary-clinton-interview-21-revealing-quotes/story?id=24064953

Gray, Peter. "Hillary Clinton's and My Wonderful Childhoods." *Psychology Today,* July 22, 2009, http://www.psychologytoday.com/blog/freedom-learn/200907/hillary-clinton-s-and-my-wonderful-childhoods

Greve, Joan. "Hillary Clinton's Decision Time." *Time,* September 19, 2014. http://time.com/3058912/hillary-clinton-2016-presidential-race-announcement/

"Hillary and Bill: 'Immediate Attraction.' " ABC News, June 9, 2003. http://abcnews.go.com/2020/story?id=123702

Kennedy Space Center. "NASA—1960s: From Dream to Reality in 10 Years." June 29, 2012. http://www.nasa.gov/centers/kennedy/about/history/timeline/60s-decade.html

Kroft, Steve. "Obama and Clinton: The 60 Minutes Interview." CBS News, January 28, 2013. http://www.cbsnews.com/news/obama-and-clinton-the-60-minutes-interview/

Nagourney, Adam, and Mark Leibovich. "Clinton Ends Campaign with Clear Call to Elect Obama." *The New York Times,* June 8, 2008. http://www.nytimes.com/2008/06/08/us/politics/08dems.html?adxnnl=1&ref=politics&adxnnlx=1418493833-HHCcV8LopCrt3z7AweOGRA

Oberg, James. "'We Don't Take Girls'" Hillary Clinton and her NASA Letter." *The Space Review,* June 10, 2013. http://www.thespacereview.com/article/2310/1

Parnes, Amie. "Hillary Clinton Puts Women's Rights at Center of her Agenda." *The Hill,* September 27, 2014. http://thehill.com/homenews/campaign/219058-hillary-clinton-puts-womens-rights-at-center-of-her-agenda

Roberts, John. "Hillary Clinton Launches White House Bid: 'I'm In.' " CNN, January 22, 2007. http://www.cnn.com/2007/POLITICS/01/20/clinton.announcement/index.html?eref=yahoo

Swaine, Jon. "Hillary Clinton Advises Women to Take Criticism 'Seriously but Not Personally.'" *The Guardian,* February 13, 2014. http://www.theguardian.com/world/2014/feb/13/hillary-clinton-melinda-gates-women-criticism

Trot, Jon. "Hillary Clinton to Wyoming: 'My Best Job Was Sliming Fish.' " *Blue Christian on the Red Background,* March 8, 2008. http://bluechristian.blogspot.com/2008/03/hillary-clinton-to-wyoming-my-best-job.html

Vagianos, Alanna. "The Hillary Clinton Guide to Being an Empowered Woman." *Huffington Post,* March 19, 2014. http://www.huffingtonpost.com/2014/03/04/hillary-clinton-quotes-lisa-rogak_n_4770130.html

White House History: The First Ladies, "Hillary Clinton." http://www.whitehousehistory.org/history/white-house-first-ladies/first-lady-hillary-clinton.html

Books

Abrams, Dennis. *Hillary Rodham Clinton: Politician.* Chelsea House, 2009.

Burgan, Michael. *Hillary Clinton.* Raintree, 2014.

Carosella, Melissa. *Hillary Clinton: First Lady, Senator, and Secretary of State.* Teacher Created Materials, 2011.

Doak, Robin S. *Hillary Clinton.* New York: Scholastic, 2013.

Guernsey, Joann Bren. *Hillary Rodham Clinton: Secretary of State.* Twenty-First Century Press, 2009.

Mapua, Jeff. *Hillary Clinton: America's Most Influential Female Politician.* Rosen Publishing, 2015.

Web Sites

The Clinton Foundation
https://www.clintonfoundation.org/

Hillary Clinton biography from Bio.com
http://www.biography.com/people/hillary-clinton-9251306

Hillary Clinton biography from Mr. Nussbaum! Learning + Fun
http://mrnussbaum.com/hillary-clinton/

White House History: The First Ladies, "Hillary Clinton"
http://www.whitehousehistory.org/history/white-house-first-ladies/first-lady-hillary-clinton.html

Glossary

assassinate (ah-SAS-ih-nayt)—To kill a famous or politically well-known person.

commencement (kuh-MENTS-ment)—Graduation ceremony.

concede (kun-SEED)—To acknowledge an opponent's victory.

dissident (DIH-sih-dent)—A person who disagrees with the methods or goals of a political party or government

FLOTUS (FLOH-tus)—First Lady of the United States.

goodwill ambassador (am-BAA-suh-dur)—A person who travels to other countries to show good will and sometimes to spread information about an organization.

impeachment (im-PEECH-ment)—The presentation of formal charges of misconduct against a public official.

nominee (nah-muh-NEE)—A person chosen to run for elective office.

overt (oh-VERT)—Open or obvious.

POTUS (POH-tus)—President of the United States.

resign (ree-ZYN)—To formally give up a position or job.

Tamra Orr has been writing books for readers of all ages for more than 20 years. She is a graduate of Ball State University and the author of more than 400 books. She works extensively in the educational assessment field, and has written magazine columns, newspaper articles, and even board game cards. Tamra and her family moved to Oregon in 2001 and have been exploring the beautiful state ever since, enjoying everything from the sandy beaches to the snowy mountaintops. When Tamra is not writing books, she is writing letters or reading books—often while camping.